D1001571

SMART GREEN CIVILIZATIONS

ANCIENT EGYPT

Perfection Learning®

Ancient Egypt

by Benita Sen

Illustrated by Yatindra Kumar

Author: Benita Sen
Managing Editor: Anupama Jauhry
Series Editor: Arshi Ahmad
Editor: Rupak Ghosh
Creative Head: Priyabrata Roy Chowdhury
Illustration Head: Yatindra Kumar
Colouring Artists: Neeraj Riddlan and Vijay Nipane
Image Research: Yukti Garg
Production Head: T Radhakrishnan
Prepress: Mahfooz Alam

Printed in the United States of America

Perfection Learning® Corporation
1000 North Second Avenue
P.O. Box 500
Logan, Iowa 51546-0500
Tel: 1-800-831-4190 • Fax: 1-800-543-2745
perfectionlearning.com

1 2 3 4 5 6 7 PP 15 14 13 12 11 10
PP/Logan, Iowa, USA
10/10/340930

RLB ISBN-13: 978-1-61563-809-3
RLB ISBN-10: 1-61563-809-1

PB ISBN-13: 978-1-61563-803-1
PB ISBN-10: 1-61563-803-2

Contents

Teri Gets a Royal Invitation!

Like most ancient civilizations, the story of ancient Egypt revolves around a river. Around 3,100 B.C., King Menes brought together Upper and Lower Egypt. Ancient Egypt grew along the Nile River and became one strong kingdom.

Most of the land was barren desert called the *Red Land*. However, strips on both sides of the Nile were called the *Black Land*.

The Nile rises in central Africa. It flows north to the Mediterranean Sea. Every spring, the Nile flooded its banks. When the floodwater left, a deposit of fertile black silt remained on the banks. This area of rich soil was about 5–10 miles wide on each side of the river. It was called the *Nile Valley*.

One evening, Teri sat up in bed with a jigsaw puzzle of the world. She was sleepy. But she just had one piece left. It was Africa.

Was she woozy with sleep? Or did Africa really look like a beautiful queen?

Before she could decide if she was awake or dreaming, she found herself in a strange house. Four ancient Egyptians announced, "Her majesty, Queen Nefertiti has invited you!"

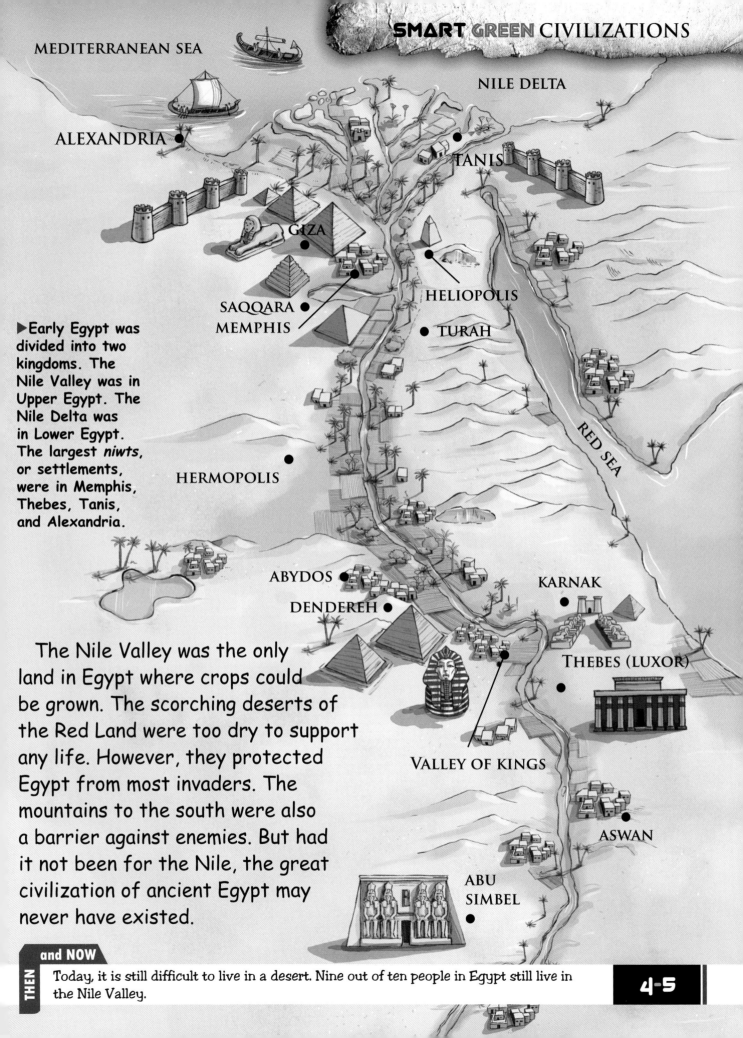

MEDITERRANEAN SEA

NILE DELTA

ALEXANDRIA

TANIS

GIZA

HELIOPOLIS

SAQQARA
MEMPHIS

TURAH

▶Early Egypt was
divided into two
kingdoms. The
Nile Valley was in
Upper Egypt. The
Nile Delta was
in Lower Egypt.
The largest *niwts*,
or settlements,
were in Memphis,
Thebes, Tanis,
and Alexandria.

HERMOPOLIS

RED SEA

ABYDOS

KARNAK

DENDEREH

THEBES (LUXOR)

The Nile Valley was the only
land in Egypt where crops could
be grown. The scorching deserts of
the Red Land were too dry to support
any life. However, they protected
Egypt from most invaders. The
mountains to the south were also
a barrier against enemies. But had
it not been for the Nile, the great
civilization of ancient Egypt may
never have existed.

VALLEY OF KINGS

ASWAN

ABU
SIMBEL

THEN and NOW

Today, it is still difficult to live in a desert. Nine out of ten people in Egypt still live in
the Nile Valley.

4-5

Cool, Ancient Homes

Welcome to ancient Egypt.

What a grand building!

Ours is an old civilization. But we were good builders. So there's still lots to see after thousands of years.

Ancient Egyptians built homes using materials available in the region. Clay from the banks of the Nile and sand were mixed with straw. This was sunbaked into bricks.

Egypt is mostly desert, and wood was hard to find. The sunbaked bricks were used instead of baking bricks in a wood kiln.

Many houses were built on platforms. This kept them above floodwaters.

Windows were built up high. Hot air rises and cool air descends. So the windows drew in cool air and let warm air escape. The high windows also kept out sand. Doors were built 4 feet above the street to keep sand out. Steps led up to the doors.

◄Ancient Egyptian homes had high walls and flat roofs. Most had a courtyard. This is where cattle, goats, and chicken were kept.

GREEN GEM Buildings made of mud or clay bricks do not harm the environment when they are destroyed. The natural materials blend with the soil.

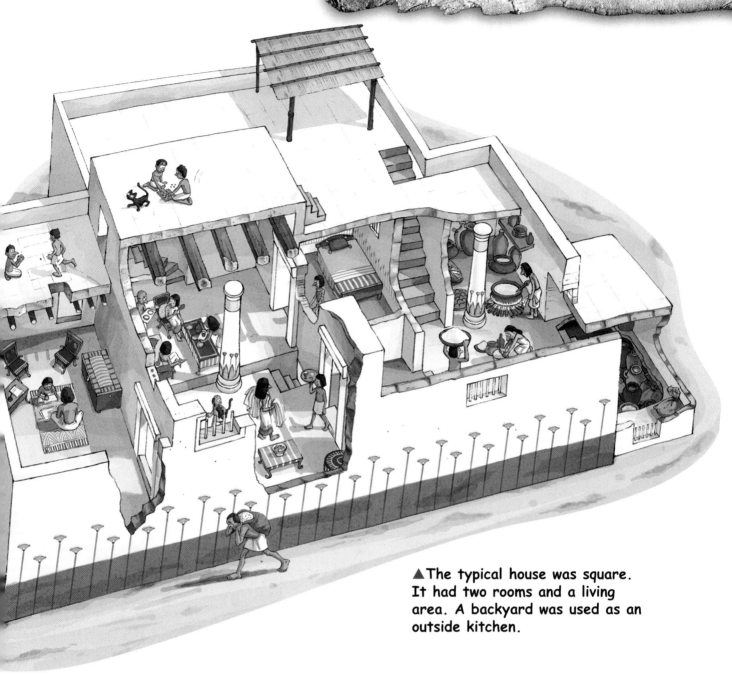

▲The typical house was square. It had two rooms and a living area. A backyard was used as an outside kitchen.

Houses were whitewashed with lime to keep them cool. They were coated with a natural paint of clay, natural colors, and a milk product called *casein*.

Since Egypt gets little rain, houses had flat, straw-covered roofs. Children played on the roof. Families would go up in the evening to catch the cool breeze or have dinner. The roofs had vents directing cool breezes into the house.

Most homes had a millstone to grind grain. They also had a silo for storing wheat and a hearth for baking bread.

THEN and NOW

Natural materials were used in ancient Egyptian houses. They did not harm the environment. Modern homes are made of synthetic materials that can harm our health.

6-7

Dress Up Like an Egyptian Queen

Ancient Egyptians dressed to stay cool in the hot Egyptian weather. They wore loose, light, comfortable clothes.

Ancient Egyptian textiles were mostly made of linen. This comes from the flax plant. Textiles were also made from sheep's wool, goat hair, palm fibers, grass, and reeds.

What a beautiful headdress and necklace!

Would you like to dress up like a little Egyptian princess?

Great costume for my next fancy party!

◄Ancient Egyptians loved to dress up. They were fond of jewelry made of gold, glass, and stone. They even believed that some jewelry could protect them.

GREEN GEM Cotton was not grown in ancient Egypt. It was introduced much later. Today, Egypt is known for its high-quality cotton.

The Egyptians were experts at beating out the flax plant to get different qualities of fiber for linen. Peasants wore coarse linen. Nobles used fine linen. Handmade linen was so fine, it could be pulled through a ring.

Women spun thread and wove it into cloth. The cloth was made into a dress by cutting it with knives of stone or metal. Then it was stitched with a needle of bone, metal, or wood.

The Egyptians were serious about hygiene and looking good. They didn't have running water. So they bathed in the Nile with soap and dabbed on perfume after a bath.

They lined their eyes with a black powder called *kohl*. They loved to fix their hair and wear wigs. They dyed gray hair with leaves of the henna plant. Younger children had their hair shaved off except for a sidelock. This kept them cool and free of lice.

▲Dressmaking was mostly done by women. They also did embroidery.

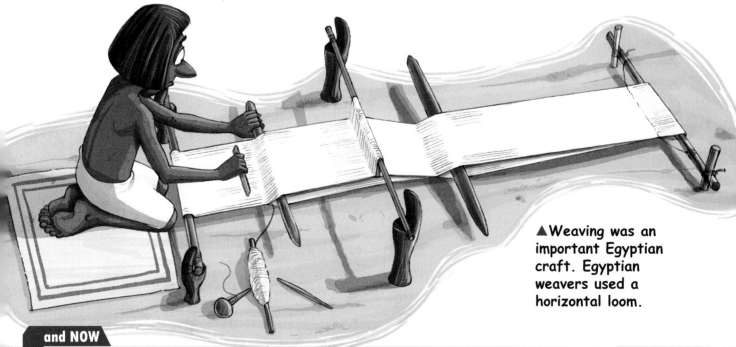

▲Weaving was an important Egyptian craft. Egyptian weavers used a horizontal loom.

THEN and NOW

Egyptians ground the leaves of the henna plant for hair dye. Many modern hair dyes are made with chemicals that can cause skin infection, hair damage, lead poisoning, and even blindness.

Could you grow food in the desert? Did you have to buy food from other countries like we do today?

No, we were perhaps the earliest farmers.

Food and Farming

The Egyptians began growing food between 10,000 B.C. and 5,200 B.C. Farming was difficult. Most of the land was sandy and dry. The soil by the Nile was like clay. It hardened when the water dried. So the Egyptians learned to plow and hoe. They grew most of what they ate.

Farmers raised grains such as wheat and barley. They grew vegetables—onions, cucumbers, cabbage, garlic, and beans.

Trees provided shade and gave fruits such as pomegranates and figs. People grew vines for melons and grapes.

◄Ancient Egyptians depended on farmers for their food. Farmers helped the civilization grow and prosper.

►Farmworkers used sickle-shaped fans to remove the husk from the grains.

GREEN GEM Egyptian farmers used hoofed animals to tramp seeds into the soil. This cut down their work while planting.

◄The Nile provided the Egyptians with fish.

The Egyptians were probably the first to keep bees. Honey was used in bread, cakes, and wine.

Grain was eaten as porridge, baked into bread, or fermented into beer. Fiber crops like flax were grown for linen cloth, as well as for oil. Sesame and castor were also pressed for oil. Using simple technology, Egyptians grew enough for all.

The floods watered the fields for about 45 days. Then when there was very little rain, farmers trapped rainwater in mud-brick tanks. They studied the slope and dug canals to their fields. In dry weather, they released water from the tanks into canals with a *shaduf*, or a pole with a bucket.

People hunted with bows and arrows, spears, and nets. The Nile provided fish. Feasts were held throughout the year.

THEN and NOW

The Egyptians salted and sun-dried fish to eat when there were few fish to catch. They did not add chemicals as is done in many modern food preservation processes today.

Achoooo!

Excuse me!

Our doctors said you get sick when you haven't been good.

Ancient Science and Wisdom

The Egyptians sought knowledge in science, math, medicine, and technology. They were among the first to study decimals in math. They knew how to add, subtract, multiply, and divide. They knew algebra and geometry. They could write numbers up to a million.

They built using the concept of ratio. They calculated how high the floodwaters were going to rise. They even used a Nilometer to measure the height of the flood.

◄Only scribes and priests knew how to read and write.

I	1
II	2
III	3
IIII	4
IIIII	5
III III	6
IIII III	7
IIII IIII	8
IIIII IIII	9
∩	10
ℓ	100
ℓ	1000
⌐	10 000
⌐	100 000
⌐	1000 000

GREEN GEM Egyptians believed herbs were healthy. Garlic and onion were taken regularly. Today, scientists have proven that garlic is good for the heart and blood pressure.

▼Ancient Egyptians were famous for their shipbuilding. The largest ancient ship ever found was from the Giza pyramid complex.

◄Egyptian doctors were highly respected in the ancient world.

Egyptian doctors believed illness was caused by bad behavior or negative spirits. Wearing a piece of jewelry called an *amulet* was one way to calm the spirits. If the patient improved, the spirit had left and the doctor began medicines.

Some doctors were surgeons. They could amputate limbs and stitch wounds. Imhotep was a well-known doctor in ancient Egypt. He is also known as a designer of pyramids.

Most physicians in ancient Egypt were also priests. They believed that different gods influenced different organs of the body.

Mining was an important industry. Thousands of workers dug out copper ores and even gold from the desert.

Boats were an important mode of travel on the Nile. By 3,000 B.C., Egyptians knew how to treat wood and build ships. One wooden ship has survived 5,000 years!

THEN and NOW

The Egyptians were the first to work out that one year has 365 days. Unlike our calendar, theirs had 10-day weeks and three weeks in a month. Each year had three four-month seasons.

12-13

Look carefully. These are Egyptian hieroglyphs. We used these in place of alphabets.

Is this a secret message?

▼Hieroglyphics were carved into stone or drawn onto papyrus parchment.

The Write Words

Hieroglyphs were the pictures that made up ancient Egyptian writing. One of the Egyptian gods was Thoth. The Egyptians believed he was the god of learning and writing. So, modern historians call the script *hieroglyphics*, or "sacred writing."

In 1799, Captain Pierre Bouchard found the Rosetta Stone. It had the same message in three different ancient writing systems. This helped historians decipher hieroglyphs.

Hieroglyphs date back to at least 3300 B.C. There were more than 6,000 symbols. Not everyone could learn to write them. So a group of people called *scribes* wrote everything. Priests, however, wrote religious texts.

▼The Egyptians believed that the god Thoth invented writing. They called the hieroglyphic script *mdwt ntr*, or "god's words."

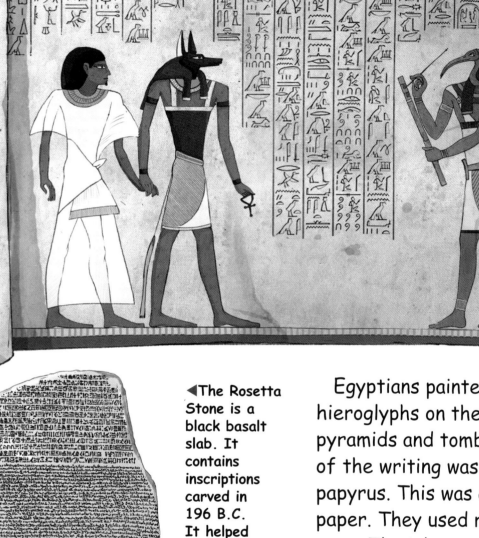

◄The Rosetta Stone is a black basalt slab. It contains inscriptions carved in 196 B.C. It helped historians read Egyptian hieroglyphs. This helped them understand ancient Egyptian civilization.

Egyptians painted hieroglyphs on the walls of pyramids and tombs. But most of the writing was done on papyrus. This was a kind of paper. They used reeds for pens. The ink was made from plants.

Hieroglyphs could be written from left to right, from right to left, or from top to bottom. It took a long time to write and learn hieroglyphs.

THEN and NOW

Papyrus paper was made from the papyrus plant. No trees had to be cut down. Today, about 93 percent of paper is made from trees.

Preparing for the Next Life

How do I look in this Egyptian costume?

You look funny! Only the dead were mummified!

The Egyptians were led by a king, or pharaoh. The word *pharaoh* means "Great House." Because the pharaoh was king, he lived in the largest house. When a pharaoh died, his chosen son often became the next king.

The pharaoh was the most important priest. He led prayers and built temples. The pharaoh owned the land. He collected taxes, made laws, and led the army.

Early Egyptians buried their dead in pits. The scorching sun, hot sand, and dry climate dried up the bodies into natural mummies. But wild animals tried to dig up the bodies. So, the Egyptians made wooden coffins for their kings.

◀The mummy of Tutankhamun, the boy king, was placed inside a gold coffin. It was decorated with colored glass and precious stones.

▶The body was embalmed using oils and salt. Internal organs were removed with instruments.

GREEN GEM Crowns and headdresses have not been found in the tombs. That's because they were made of organic, biodegradable materials.

▼The long process of embalming and drying lasted about 40 days. The body was then wrapped in strips of linen to make a mummy.

To prevent their kings' bodies from decaying in coffins, Egyptians mummified, or preserved, their royals after cleaning the body.

All organs but the heart were removed. The body was stuffed with linen and sawdust so it didn't lose shape. The mummy was placed in a coffin. The coffin went inside a pyramid of mud, limestone, and granite. Ornaments, jars, clothes, and food, thought to be needed in the afterlife, were left there too.

THEN and NOW

Hatshepsut, the first woman Pharaoh, dressed like a man. She even wore a fake beard! Today, many women are becoming leaders. They no longer need to dress like a man!

Towering Over the Dead

The first pyramids, or *mastabas*, were made during the Third Dynasty, around 2,681 B.C. The steps symbolized the journey to heaven. Even-sided pyramids came later.

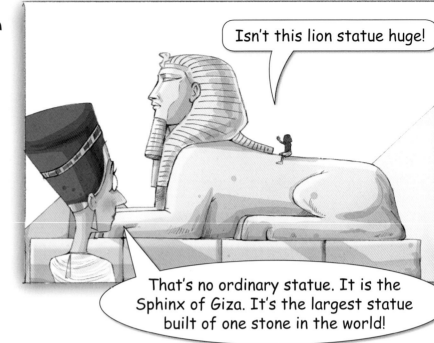

Isn't this lion statue huge!

That's no ordinary statue. It is the Sphinx of Giza. It's the largest statue built of one stone in the world!

Over the next thousand years, more than a hundred pyramids were built. Egyptians were expert builders. Even the early pyramids had many chambers, or rooms.

The walls of pyramids were painted with scenes from daily life. The earliest pyramids were square buildings with a room for the mummy. Next came the tombs made from a mound of earth. Then came the pointed pyramids at Giza.

▼Egyptian architects and masons made plans before building the pyramids.

GREEN GEM The Egyptians painted pottery with natural colors. Green and blue were from copper. Red was from iron. Silver was mixed for yellow, and manganese gave them purple.

Sphinxes are stone statues of resting lions with human heads. They guard the temples and pyramids. Later, important roads leading to pyramids were lined with dozens of sphinxes.

Egypt had some of the most skilled craftsmen. They often worked in workshops. They made things for daily use, for temples, or for pyramids.

Cities of workmen like Deir el-Medina, Kahun, and Giza grew where a new pyramid was built. Craftsmen were so respected for their skills that when they died, they were buried in decorated tombs.

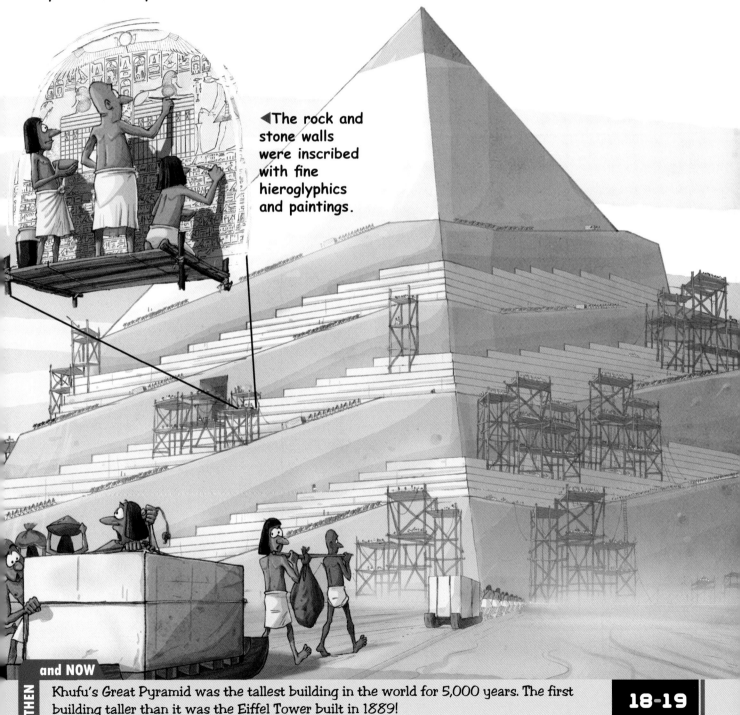

◄The rock and stone walls were inscribed with fine hieroglyphics and paintings.

and NOW

THEN Khufu's Great Pyramid was the tallest building in the world for 5,000 years. The first building taller than it was the Eiffel Tower built in 1889!

18-19

Lots of Work to Be Done

The pharaoh was the most important person in Egypt. His closest friends were a handful of nobles and their families, priests, and government officials. Next in importance were scribes, teachers, soldiers, doctors, and some craftsmen. Most of the common people were farmers, servants, and unskilled craftsmen. Slaves were usually people from other countries.

What kind of pyramid is that?

Oh, that shows how our society was organized. The king and queen are at the top. The slaves are at the bottom.

▶Ancient Egyptian society was divided into classes. The groups of people nearest the top of society were the richest and most powerful.

Workers' colonies had drainage and sewage systems. This kept the colonies clean and the workers in good health.

Priests could be teachers and scribes. Scribes recorded taxes, the season's harvest, wages, and other details for the pharaoh. So they were an important part of the government. They also had to know mathematics to calculate. They were respected for being so learned.

Ordinary people kept busy throughout the year. They had to do most of their own work.

Boys from rich homes went to school when they were barely four. Boys learned to write and calculate. They also studied astronomy and law. It was important for them to learn some sports like gymnastics and to be good people.

Most boys grew up to help their fathers. So sons of scribes and priests often took up their father's work. They studied for many years. Children of farmers learned to work the fields and look after farm animals.

Girls grew up to help their mother. Most girls didn't go to school. They were taught a little at home by a slave or by the mother. They married around the age of 15.

THEN and NOW
Unlike in today's cities, most houses in ancient Egypt were built by the people who lived in them. Houses were simple and wasted fewer resources.

20-21

Time to Spare

Most Egyptians worked hard, but they found time for fun. Around 3,500 B.C., they made a game called *Senet*. The game was played on a board made from stone, mud, or wood.

Senet was played by two people and stood for the passage of life from birth to death. It was so popular that four Senet boards were buried with Pharaoh Tutankhamun.

The Egyptian climate was warm. So children spent a lot of time outdoors. They enjoyed swimming, dancing, riding donkeys, and playing leapfrog and tug-of-war.

Egyptian children played with rag dolls; toy animals; tops; and balls made of papyrus, cloth, and leather. They kept cats, birds, and monkeys as pets.

We worked hard and had fun!

I love your game. Tell me more about your pastimes.

▶Ancient Egyptians danced in groups. They played music on harps and other stringed instruments.

 GREEN GEM Fitness was important to the Egyptians. They boxed and fenced. They were good athletes. The pharaoh participated in a marathon race at the Heb Sed festival to prove he was fit to rule.

◄Ancient Egyptians played board games with counters and dice.

Children also had carved wooden toys with moveable parts. Toy animals had glass eyes with moveable legs. Some had tails that wagged or a mouth that opened and closed when the toy was pulled along.

The Egyptians loved to dance. Dancers; musicians on harps, flutes, and lutes; and singers were popular at festivals. Drummers kept the beat.

Egyptians celebrated marriages and festivals with feasts. Different types of food and wine were served. Guests were welcomed with lotus flowers.

THEN and NOW
All the Egyptian games and toys were made of natural materials. Today, many toys and games are made of harmful plastics and require batteries or electric power.

Children of Many Gods

Everything the Egyptians did was influenced by their religion. They worshiped many gods and goddesses. They prayed for protection.

The Egyptians believed the world rose from a dark ocean. Then Ra, the sun god, came up from a blue lotus and lit the earth.

Is that a man, a beast, or a god?

That's Ra, the sun god. He created the world. The rising sun was the symbol of creation for us.

▼Ancient Egyptians were very religious people. They believed in many gods and goddesses.

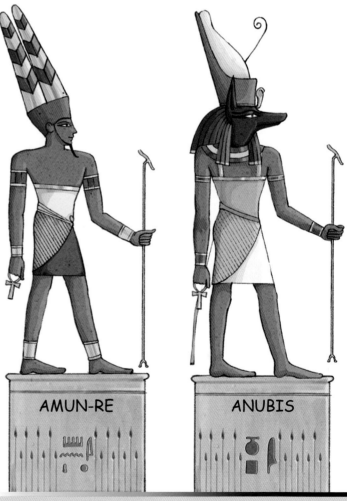

THOTH

OSIRIS

AMUN-RE

ANUBIS

Egyptians were the first to domesticate the cat about 4,000 years ago. They believed cats to be sacred and treated them with kindness.

Some of the earliest gods were in the shape of animals. Others were part-human, part-animal. Ra, Horus, and Thoth all had the heads of birds. Anubis had the head of a jackal.

Amun-Re was the combination of Amun, the god of creation, and Ra (or Re), the sun god. He was considered the king of gods.

Each god had a different role. Some brought the floods. Others took over the dead or protected towns.

Some gods were only worshiped by priests or other important people in temples where the statue was kept. Ordinary people did not go to the temple. Instead, the statue of the god was brought out for worship on festival days.

Homes had niches in the walls for holy statues. Families lit lamps and incense in honor of the gods. Animals were sacrificed to make the gods happy.

▶Ra, the sun god, was the most important god of ancient Egyptians. He had the body of a human and the head of a falcon. He had a sun disk on his head.

and NOW

THEN

Sacred animals like the cat were protected by law in ancient Egypt. Even today, some countries have laws to protect animals.

End of Glory

It is not clear how the glorious civilization of ancient Egypt ended. The end was not sudden. For centuries, the vast Sahara Desert to its west protected Egypt from raiders. But the Egyptians fought among themselves.

Sometimes, enemies attacked from Libya, to the west of Egypt. The Nubians to the south fought the Egyptians. From 690–664 B.C., Egyptian King Taharqa fought the Assyrians. The Assyrians raided important Egyptian cities like Thebes.

Why did your civilization disappear?

Everything must come to an end. So did our civilization. Perhaps one day you will find out what exactly caused our end.

GREEN GEM — Even though houses were made of mud, entire villages of ancient Egypt still stand. These include Deir el-Medina, Mirgissa, and the Buhen Fort.

▼Internal wars and foreign invaders tore ancient Egypt apart. They gradually brought the civilization to an end.

With successive invasions, the original religion and beliefs died out. Egypt slowly began to lose its identity. So did their writing.

Some historians believe that Egypt's progress suffered because there were no iron ore mines. Any iron they used had to be bought from abroad. That made it expensive.

So Egyptians were late in using iron weapons. In the battle at Qadesh with Turkey, the Egyptians used bronze. It is mainly made of copper and is not as strong as iron. This put Egyptian soldiers at a disadvantage.

The Romans took over Egypt in 30 B.C. They made Egypt a part of their empire. The Persians, Greeks, and Arabs also attacked the country. Each raid weakened Egypt. Finally, almost 3,000 years after it began, the glorious ancient civilization of Egypt ended.

THEN and NOW
Egypt draws millions of tourists every year. Experts believe pollution caused by tourism is ruining many monuments.

Keep this papyrus roll with you. The story of my civilization is written here.

Thanks! You've been a wonderful guide! Egypt has come alive for me.

Green Lessons

■ The Egyptians built with local materials. Limestone, sandstone, and granite were used for monuments.

■ Homes and palaces were made of mud bricks. These kept the buildings much cooler than stone.

■ The Great Pyramid of Giza was built around 2,580 B.C. It is one of the seven ancient wonders of the world. It still stands today. This serves as an example of Egypt's mighty construction.

■ Egyptians did not have machines and trucks to move materials. But they developed simple machines. Heavy things like stones were moved with levers. Using the advantage of a slope, they moved materials up and down ramps. Boxes were shifted on rollers, or wheels.